C000177436

GLENN WALDRON

Originally from Plymouth, Glenn Waldron was editor of influential style magazine *i-D* from 2004 to 2006. Since then, his work has been featured in publications including *Vogue*, *The New York Times*, *W* magazine, *Guardian* and *Independent*, and he has taught journalism at the London College of Fashion. Other theatre credits include *Plucky* (Bush Theatre/DryWrite), and a piece for Come To Where I'm From (Paines Plough).

Other Titles in this Series

Glenn Waldron

FOREVER HOUSE

NICK HERN BOOKS

London

www.nickhernbooks.co.uk

A Nick Hern Book

Forever House first published in Great Britain as a paperback original in 2013 by Nick Hern Books Limited, The Glasshouse, 49a Goldhawk Road, London W12 8QP, in association with the Drum Theatre Plymouth

Forever House copyright © 2013 Glenn Waldron

Glenn Waldron has asserted his right to be identified as the author of this work

Cover photograph: Robin Maddock
Cover design: Ned Hoste, 2H

Typeset by Nick Hern Books, London
Printed in the UK by Mimeo Ltd, Huntingdon, Cambridgeshire PE29 6XX

A CIP catalogue record for this book is available from the British Library

ISBN 978 1 84842 330 5

Forever House was first performed at the Drum Theatre
Plymouth, on 21 March 2013, with the following cast:

RICHARD	Dylan Kennedy
GRAHAM	Tom Peters
LAURA	Leah Whitaker
BECCI	Becci Gemmell
LUCY	Joana Nastari
MARK	Tom Andrews

Director	Joe Murphy
Set & Costume Designer	Hannah Clark
Lighting Designer	Malcolm Rippeth
Sound Designer	Isobel Waller-Bridge
Assistant Director	Bethany Pitts
Casting Director	Charlotte Sutton
Dialect Coach	Mary Howland
Production Manager	Nick Soper
Stage Manager	Sarah Caselton-Smith
Deputy Stage Manager	Kelsi Lewis
Assistant Stage Manager	April Lindsay
Props Supervisor	Kate Holliday
Costume Supervisor	Lorna Price
Drum Technician	Matt Hoyle
Sets, props and costumes	TR2, Theatre Royal Plymouth Production Centre

Produced by	Drum Theatre Plymouth
Artistic Director	Simon Stokes

Acknowledgements

Joe Murphy, Simon Stokes, David Prescott and everyone at
Theatre Royal Plymouth, Bethany Pitts, Hannah Clark, Isobel
Waller-Bridge, Charlotte Sutton and our incredible cast and
crew. Harriet Pennington Legh at Troika, James Grieve and
Paines Plough, Robin Maddock, Rob Drummer, Rachael
Stevens, Phoebe Waller-Bridge, the man in Peverell who
initially thought David Prescott and I were burglars but then
very kindly showed us round his house, Matt Hall at the Marine
Biological Association, my friends and family.

G.W.

For Tom and Wilf

Characters

RICHARD, *a young man*
GRAHAM, *forty-five*
LAURA, *twenty-eight*
BECCI, *twenty-eight*
LUCY, *twenty-three*
MARK, *thirty-nine*

Note on Text

/ *indicates an interruption in dialogue.*

[ ] *indicates when a word is implied but not said.*

… *indicates an unfinished or unarticulated thought.*

– *indicates a very brief pause or a beat where a thought is being clarified.*

A beat is a bit longer than that. A pause is a bit longer still.
A long pause is longer still and pretty much unbearable.

This text went to press before the end of rehearsals and so may differ slightly from the play as performed.

One

September 1999. The living room of a Victorian terraced house in Plymouth, not particularly near the sea. It's early evening – there's still a bit of light coming in from outside. The room has a rather elegant corniced ceiling and a cheap-looking carpet. There's a leather sofa, an armchair and a record player, along with some large cardboard boxes and haphazard stacks of books and records. Up against the wall are various prints and framed exhibition posters, waiting to be hung. A recording of Mozart piano sonatas plays in the background.

A young man, RICHARD, *is sat on the edge of the sofa. He still has his jacket and rucksack on. He seems uncertain of his surroundings. There's an almost-painful self-awareness to everything he does.*

A man's voice (GRAHAM) *from the kitchen.*

GRAHAM (*off*). The Contax S2. Have you seen that?

RICHARD. Yes, I think so. (*Beat.*) Maybe. (*Beat.*) I don't know.

GRAHAM (*off*). Same kind of thing as the Canon I think but with a Carl Zeiss lens. You should check it out.

RICHARD. Um. Okay.

A pause. RICHARD *takes his rucksack off and places it on the sofa next to him. He thinks about it for several moments then moves it slightly. The position seems somehow important.*

GRAHAM (*off*). Remind me what you have again.

RICHARD. Er, nothing really.

GRAHAM (*off*). Sorry?

RICHARD (*louder*). A – er – an Olympus OM-1?

GRAHAM (*off*). That's alright.

RICHARD. It's not but – but I'm saving up.

GRAHAM (*off*). Are you?

RICHARD. Yes.

GRAHAM (*off*). What for?

RICHARD. Um. A Minolta Dynax 700si?

GRAHAM (*off*). Sorry?

RICHARD. A Minolta Dynax?

GRAHAM (*off*). Oh, great. The 500 or the 600?

RICHARD. The, um, 700?

GRAHAM (*off*). Wow, fantastic. How far have you got to go?

RICHARD. Oh, um. A bit. (*Beat.*) I could buy the 600 now but I'm gonna wait.

GRAHAM (*off*). Good for you. No point in skimping. Would you like some nibbles?

RICHARD. Um, no? (*He does.*) No. I'm fine, thank you.

GRAHAM (*off*). Are you sure?

RICHARD. Yes? (*He's not.*) Yes, thank you.

Another pause. RICHARD *thinks then moves the rucksack again, this time putting it on the floor to the side of the sofa.*

GRAHAM (*off*). Used to have a 9xi. Do you know it?

RICHARD. Um. No.

GRAHAM (*off*). Quite heavy but brilliant shutter speed. Stopped making them now I think. Shame really.

GRAHAM *enters. He has a relaxed, fatherly appearance. He is fairly tall; ruggedly handsome though slightly gone to seed. He has just-greying hair and some facial stubble. He wears jeans, a jumper and a pair of socks with a hole in the toe. He's carrying two mugs of coffee and has to push the door open with his foot.*

RICHARD *jumps up when* GRAHAM *comes in the room.*

There you go.

RICHARD. Thanks.

GRAHAM. Take your coat off if you want to.

RICHARD. Oh. Yes. (*Beat*.) Um…

There is no coffee table and RICHARD *doesn't know where to put his mug.*

GRAHAM. Oh, gimme that.

RICHARD *hands* GRAHAM *his mug and then, rather awkwardly, takes his jacket off. He is aware of* GRAHAM *watching him as he does so.*

RICHARD. Um.

He now doesn't know what to do with his coat.

GRAHAM (*patient*). Swap.

RICHARD *gives* GRAHAM *his coat and takes back his coffee.*

RICHARD (*embarrassed*). Thanks.

GRAHAM. I'll just go and [hang this up].

GRAHAM *puts his own mug down on a pile of books and then goes to hang* RICHARD's *coat in the hall.* RICHARD *is not sure whether to sit back down or stay standing. He stays standing.* GRAHAM *comes back in.*

Have a seat, Richard…

RICHARD *sits down on the sofa. There's a pile of books on the armchair so* GRAHAM *sits on the floor, his back propped against the seat of the chair. It's quite a youthful gesture.*

Actually is it Richard or do you prefer Rich or?

RICHARD (*he's never been asked this before*). Um. Well. Some of the – some people call me Rich or, um, Richie, but – but actually I prefer Richard.

GRAHAM. Right.

Beat.

RICHARD. I don't think I look like a Rich.

GRAHAM. No.

RICHARD. Or a Richie.

GRAHAM. No. (*Beat.*) And definitely not a Dick.

An embarrassed laugh from RICHARD.

What's your middle name?

RICHARD (*going red*). Oh.

GRAHAM. I'm sorry. Am I being nosy? Tell me to mind my own /

RICHARD. No no, it's just. It's – Cliff – (*Looking at* GRAHAM*'s reaction.*)

GRAHAM. That's alright.

RICHARD. It's – if you think about it.

GRAHAM. Cliff. Richard Cliff. Ah.

RICHARD. My mum – big fan.

GRAHAM. I see.

RICHARD. She says I should be honoured.

GRAHAM. Maybe she's right.

RICHARD. I don't think so.

GRAHAM. No, nor do I. (*Laughs.*) Sorry.

RICHARD. No, it's…

A pause.

GRAHAM (*reminding him*). Your coffee.

RICHARD. Oh. Yes.

He picks up the mug and cautiously takes a sip.

GRAHAM. Are you sure you wouldn't like some – some biscuits or something.

RICHARD. No, I'm – I'm fine. Thanks. (*Beat.*) Unless you…

GRAHAM. Actually I don't think I've got any biscuits so… Kitchen's in a worse state than [in here]. Wouldn't think I'd been here two months already, would you? Did you find it okay?

RICHARD. Oh. Yes. I walk round here all the time.

GRAHAM. Nine New Park Road – trips off the tongue, doesn't it?

RICHARD *doesn't have anything to say to this. He shrugs and smiles.*

A pause.

Well, I'm really glad you called me, Richard. It's – it's not often you meet someone with the same interests.

Beat.

It was strange in the library, wasn't it?

RICHARD. You wanted a book on Man Ray and I had one in my bag.

GRAHAM. Yes... What were you after?

RICHARD. Sorry?

GRAHAM. In the library. What were you looking for?

RICHARD. Oh, um. I can't [remember]. I just go there sometimes and – have a look.

GRAHAM. Right, right. (*Beat.*) Photography section's pretty shocking, isn't it?

RICHARD. Um, yeah.

GRAHAM. There's, like, a copy of *Practical Photography* from the late eighties, a Cartier-Bresson monograph and a book with pictures of babies dressed up as sunflowers and vegetables.

RICHARD. Yeah.

GRAHAM. I mean, what's that about?

RICHARD. Yeah.

GRAHAM. Not exactly comprehensive.

RICHARD. Yeah.

Beat.

GRAHAM. Hey, if you're ever looking for something then – then I could get you into the library at the art college. If you wanted.

RICHARD. Um, thanks.

GRAHAM. Or you could just – you could just borrow my pass. They never check.

RICHARD. Okay. Great. (*Beat.*) Thanks.

> *Pause.* GRAHAM *drinks his coffee.* RICHARD *follows his cue and drinks his.*

GRAHAM. And what did you think of the Man Ray?

RICHARD. Oh. Um. (*Wanting to say something intelligent.*) I liked it. The pictures are – well, they're very surreal. I mean, it's Surrealism so that's a stupid thing to say but... (*Trying again.*) I liked the way they're – they don't try to make you feel anything.

GRAHAM. How do you mean?

RICHARD. It's like – it's like there's a kind of – um – deadness to them. Like Man Ray, like she doesn't really /

GRAHAM. He.

RICHARD. Um?

GRAHAM. He. Man Ray was – was a man.

RICHARD (*embarrassed*). Oh. Sorry, I /

GRAHAM. No, it's fine. I didn't mean to /

RICHARD. Stupid....

GRAHAM. No, I'm [sorry] – I should have let you... I just – I thought you'd rather know.

RICHARD. Yes. I did. I mean, I do! (*Beat.*) Thank you.

GRAHAM. So you were saying...

RICHARD. Um. Forgotten what I was going to –

GRAHAM. 'Man Ray – It's like he...'

RICHARD. Oh. Yes. It's like he – he doesn't really feel anything. I mean, there isn't any real feeling in his pictures.

GRAHAM. Okay.

RICHARD. Like the one with the teardrops, it's – it's very pretty but – it's not really sad. I mean, it's a teardrop but it's a fake teardrop so you can't really –

GRAHAM. Be moved by it?

RICHARD. Yes.

GRAHAM. Sort of like, I dunno, the memory of a teardrop?

RICHARD. Yes.

GRAHAM (*entertaining this idea*). Okay. So is he just – tricking the viewer then or?

RICHARD (*thinks*). Um, not tricking them but sort-of sort-of saying that we can't really trust what we see. Because it's a photo. It's not, like, a real sadness. We can't, um, touch it.

GRAHAM. Okay.

RICHARD. It's not, like, a sadness you can, like, feel because – because it's already in the past.

GRAHAM. Right, right. (*Beat.*) But isn't that quite sad in itself?

RICHARD (*smiles*). Yes. Maybe.

GRAHAM. Okay. (*Engaging with this.*) So what about someone like Atget then? Do you – do you think we can trust his photographs more?

RICHARD (*embarrassed*). I – I don't know who that is.

GRAHAM. That's alright.

RICHARD. Sorry.

GRAHAM. No no, it's – don't apologise.

Another pause. There's a ping-pong of awkward smiles.

Do you like this music? Is it a bit much?

RICHARD. No, I like it. I like classical music.

GRAHAM. Do you?

RICHARD. Yes.

GRAHAM. Do you know what this is?

RICHARD. Um, I think it's, like, a Mozart sonata or something.

GRAHAM. Wow.

RICHARD. I – I used to play the piano.

GRAHAM. Did you?

RICHARD. Yes. Not very well but…

GRAHAM. Do you still play?

RICHARD. Um, not really. Well – not at all. I used to have lessons with this old lady in Plymstock – Mrs Stephens? – but then I stopped going.

GRAHAM. Did you not enjoy it?

RICHARD. Not really, no. I mean, I liked playing the piano but I didn't like – she had these really long nails and every time she played the piano, they'd make this sort-of sort-of clacking sound against the keys. And her house was – not very clean.

GRAHAM. Right.

RICHARD. Is that a bad thing to say? I don't mean it in a bad way but – it really did stink of piss.

GRAHAM (*amused*). Don't worry, I won't tell anyone.

Another long pause. RICHARD *looks around the room and sneaks nervous glances at* GRAHAM.

(*A snap decision.*) Sod it, shall we have a drink?

RICHARD. Um.

GRAHAM (*getting up*). I mean a proper drink. It's Saturday night, it's been a pretty hellish week frankly and… come on, let's have a drink.

RICHARD. Um. (*Beat.*) Okay, great.

GRAHAM *goes to the kitchen.* RICHARD *just sits there for several moments.*

GRAHAM (*from the door*). So I've got wine or, er – wine.

RICHARD (*attempting a joke*). I think I'll have some wine.

GRAHAM (*laughing*). Good. (*The music has now stopped.*)
Hey, put something else on if you want.

RICHARD. Okay.

*GRAHAM goes back to the kitchen. A pause, then
RICHARD takes an inhaler out of his bag and uses it
quickly. He then gets up and tentatively looks through a pile
of records. He doesn't know what he's looking for. Anything
that catches his eye.*

*GRAHAM comes back in with a bottle of red wine, a
corkscrew and two glasses. He starts opening the bottle.*

GRAHAM (*of the record collection*). Find anything?

RICHARD. Um. I don't really...

GRAHAM. Oh I know. All prehistoric, I'm afraid. Here.

*He gives RICHARD a glass of wine. RICHARD looks at the
wine like it's a foreign object.*

Oh. I'm sorry. Do you like red? I always assume that
everyone likes red but some people don't, do they?

RICHARD. Yes – I mean, no. I suppose they don't. But – but I
do. I like wine. All wine, really.

GRAHAM. Oh, good.

A beat.

RICHARD. I mean, I'm not – I'm not a – a *wine connoisseur*
but I do – I do like it.

GRAHAM. Right. (*Beat.*) Well. Cheers.

RICHARD. Um, cheers.

*It's clear that RICHARD isn't really used to drinking wine.
He looks at the glass cautiously then takes a big gulp.
There's a bit of an awkward pause afterwards then both sit –
this time GRAHAM perches on the edge of the armchair.*

GRAHAM. So did you find anything in my sad apology for a
record collection?

RICHARD. Um. (*Flicking through.*) I like the cover of this one.
It's sort of – sort of wistful, isn't it?

GRAHAM. Lemme see.

> RICHARD *holds the record up for* GRAHAM *to see.*

> Yeah, it's very... The light on her face.

RICHARD. It sort of – because she's not really pretty – but it sort of makes her look sort-of –

GRAHAM. Yeah.

> *Beat.*

RICHARD. How – how would they do that – with the light?

GRAHAM. Let me see, it's –

> GRAHAM *reaches over and takes the record.*

> (*There's a possibility that* GRAHAM *is winging this.*) Yeah, I think it's probably natural light and then they've used, um, reflectors to bump it up and create that kind of – around the eyes. Avedon does that quite a lot. Do you know Avedon?

RICHARD. I think – I think I've heard of him. (*He hasn't.*)

GRAHAM. Oh, you should definitely check him out. Does incredible things with light.

> GRAHAM *gets up and starts looking through stacks of books.*

> *In the West. In the West*, where are you? (*Talking as he looks.*) A lot of photographers don't like Avedon all that much. Think he's a bit of whore. Taking – nope – taking Sander's ugly peasants and kind of *appropriating* them. Making them *fashionable* and – ah here...

> *He finds the book and gives the book to* RICHARD, *who starts flicking through it. A pause.*

A lot of these are pure set-ups, you know? They're not portraits of, um, really real people in their own homes. But I think that's kind of why they're fascinating, isn't it? He gives us the stories we want. Avedon's not really presenting reality but – but some kind of *half-remembered* version of it, almost like he thinks it isn't possible to capture – (*Checks himself.*) Sorry, am I going on?

RICHARD. Oh. No.

GRAHAM. Are you sure?

RICHARD. Yes.

GRAHAM. Sorry. Slipping into lecture mode. Force of habit.

RICHARD. No, it's – I'm – I'm interested.

GRAHAM. Are you?

RICHARD. Yes.

> GRAHAM *looks intently at* RICHARD.

GRAHAM. Great. (*Beat.*) So – so what do you think? About the pictures.

RICHARD. Um, I think they're really – I think they're really – really... good.

> *Beat.*

> It feels like – like there's a clarity to them.

GRAHAM. Right, right.

RICHARD. And the pictures have this kind of – they feel quite... luminous.

GRAHAM (*seeing something in him*). Yes.

> RICHARD *flicks through the book for a few moments and then shuts it.*

> Borrow it, if you like.

RICHARD. Oh. Thanks but /

GRAHAM. Please. I'd like you to.

RICHARD. No, I'm /

GRAHAM. I insist.

> *Beat.*

RICHARD. Okay. Thanks. Thank you.

GRAHAM. Graham.

RICHARD. Sorry?

GRAHAM. Thank you, Graham.

RICHARD. Oh. Yes. Thank you, Graham.

GRAHAM. You're welcome, Richard.

RICHARD *doesn't know what to do with the book now. He decides to put the book in his rucksack. There's something quite childlike about this action.*

And how's *your* work coming on, Richard?

RICHARD. Um?

GRAHAM. Your photography.

RICHARD. Oh.

RICHARD *is a bit flustered.*

GRAHAM. What?

RICHARD. Nothing, it's just –

GRAHAM. What have I said?

RICHARD. No, it's just – I'm not exactly – I'm not really a photographer.

GRAHAM. Are you not?

RICHARD. No. (*Beat.*) I mean I take pictures but…

GRAHAM. But what?

RICHARD. But they're not really of… It's just, like, ordinary things. Things I see around me.

GRAHAM. Like what?

RICHARD. Like, I dunno, just – things that… People and… (*Beat.*) There was one time when my little sister lost, like, two teeth on the same day. She had this gap in her teeth that made her look like…

GRAHAM. Okay.

RICHARD (*embarrassed*). I mean, it's not really anything that anyone would be [interested in]…

GRAHAM. Why do you say that?

RICHARD *shrugs.*

GRAHAM. You think that because you're just starting out that no one would be interested?

RICHARD. Yes. And I mean, this is – well, this is Plymouth, it's not – it's not New York or.

GRAHAM. So Plymouth isn't a worthy subject for an artist? You think Plymouth's only good for a Beryl Cook painting. Fat ladies and saucy sailors?

A laugh of recognition from RICHARD.

…You don't think Plymouth has the same things as other places? The same life and – and love and happiness and sex and, and – humanity as other places?

RICHARD (*a little awkward*). I don't [know] – I haven't really – thought about it.

Pause. RICHARD *takes a big gulp of wine. The doorbell goes. It's quite a loud, ugly noise.*

GRAHAM (*a little thrown*). Shit. (*Beat.*) Okay. Let's just [leave it].

A pause. It goes again.

Okay so – I should probably [get that].

RICHARD. I can just [go]…

GRAHAM. No, no. It's – you just – it's fine. Just – relax. Have some more wine, okay?

RICHARD. Okay.

GRAHAM *goes to the door. We overhear snatches of the conversation. It's a woman, a friend of* GRAHAM's – *he's friendly but there's a terseness to his responses and he doesn't invite her in. Meanwhile,* RICHARD *pours himself another glass of wine. He looks at it for several moments then downs it in one go. It's quite painful but he manages not to choke. He then pours himself another glass. From here on, it should be clear that* RICHARD *is, if not inebriated, then certainly heading in that direction. After the drink,* RICHARD *sits there for a while until* GRAHAM *comes back with some carrier bags of student work, which he puts down somewhere.*

GRAHAM (*rattled*). Richard, I'm really [sorry]. Just a – a work colleague dropping off some double-marking.

RICHARD *nods sagely*.

(*Starts moving the pile of books off the armchair.*) Not sure why she thought it was a good idea to do it on a Saturday night but – think she might have a bit of a [thing] or… anyway. Um. Sorry.

RICHARD. No, it's…

GRAHAM (*sitting down in the armchair*). So. So what were we [talking about]? (*Beat.*) Oh yes, your work. Have you ever shown your work to anyone?

RICHARD. Oh. Well um, not really. (*Beat.*) I, um, showed some of them to this – this teacher, the art teacher at school but – and he sort-of liked them actually. He said some of them – I mean, obviously some of them are just sort-of rubbish but – he said some of them had this – this sort-of honesty to them? And he said that was – um – that was a good quality for them to have but…

GRAHAM. And do you think he meant it?

RICHARD. Yes – I think so.

GRAHAM. Well, there you go.

Beat.

RICHARD. There's also this – competition?

GRAHAM. Right.

RICHARD. It's only for schools but – and every school in Devon and Cornwall has to – has to enter one piece of – piece of artwork. And the winner gets some book tokens or something but all the, um, all the artworks get shown in an exhibition.

GRAHAM. I see.

RICHARD. And my school – they've sort-of chosen mine.

GRAHAM. Really?

RICHARD. Yeah.

GRAHAM. Wow!

RICHARD. I mean, it's not, like /

GRAHAM. No, that's fantastic!

RICHARD. It's only a school thing but /

GRAHAM. But you're already an exhibited photographer…

RICHARD. Yeah, I /

GRAHAM. I didn't know we had an exhibited photographer in the room!

RICHARD *laughs*.

Think I need to get your autograph.

RICHARD *is a bit embarrassed by this but also pleased*.

RICHARD. It's not that big a deal.

GRAHAM. Wow, an exhibition. (*Beat*.) Hey, let's have a toast.

GRAHAM *tops up* RICHARD's *glass*.

To – um – future ambitions. Cheers.

RICHARD. Um, cheers.

For some reason, RICHARD *feels compelled to down most of his glass. Throughout the next bit of the scene, the light is fading and the room is beginning to get dark.*

GRAHAM. What was the picture?

RICHARD. Oh. It was just…

GRAHAM. What?

RICHARD. It was nothing, really.

GRAHAM. What was it?

RICHARD. It was this – a portrait. This lad. At school.

GRAHAM. Okay.

RICHARD. I've been taking pictures of him for – for a while. Sort-of documenting him, his life. It's quite silly really. Just, like, pictures of him kind-of growing up and – and maturing, I suppose.

GRAHAM. And what's this lad's name?

RICHARD. His name's Nick.

GRAHAM. And he's your mate is he – Nick?

RICHARD. Sort-of. Our mums are friends and – and we've sort of grown up together. In the church but – I mean, at school we're – we're not in the same group or anything. He plays football.

GRAHAM. And you don't?

RICHARD *laughs*.

Why's that funny?

Beat.

So your family – they're Catholic or?

RICHARD. Um, Methodist. But, like, full-on Methodist. Like, clapping and tambourines and – we go to church three times a week.

GRAHAM. Really?

RICHARD. Yes.

GRAHAM. Crumbs. And do you do all that – do you speak in tongues and – what's it called – the falling-over thingy.

RICHARD. The Toronto blessing, yes. Some people do. I mean, I've seen them doing it.

GRAHAM. It all seems very strange to me.

RICHARD. Yes. I mean, it doesn't seem strange to me but then it's very… Sometimes I'll – sometimes I'll look at what they're doing and I sort of think 'blimey, what's that about', you know?

GRAHAM. Yes.

RICHARD. There's this one woman – Jean Goodacre – and – and even my mum and dad think she's a bit loopy. One time, she came up to my little sister and she told her that she had this, um, vision? And I was sort-of in this vision. I was in this place that – it wasn't a good place and – there was sort-of these – these black altars and there was kind of like

goblins on them and – and I was on one of these altars and…
(*An awkward laugh.*) yeah.

GRAHAM. Fuck.

RICHARD. Yeah.

GRAHAM. And what did you – what did your sister say to that?

RICHARD. I don't – I don't think she said anything. But she
told my mum and she went ballistic. They don't speak to
Jean Goodacre any more.

Pause.

GRAHAM. And what about you? Do you 'have faith'?

Beat.

RICHARD. I think so. I mean, definitely some of it. But then
other stuff, I'm not… but it's not like they let you believe
some bits and then not the others. At my church. It's totally –
um – *total*, you know?

GRAHAM. Right.

RICHARD. I like, like, the Psalms and I like taking
communion.

GRAHAM. Right.

RICHARD. But then some of the music is – I think it's a right
din sometimes and – and just a bit rubbish really – and then I
sort-of think 'well, if I think it's rubbish then, then why
would God want to listen to it?' Does that sound silly?

GRAHAM (*a laugh*). No, not at all.

Pause.

RICHARD. Do you – do you believe in God?

GRAHAM. No.

Pause. They are suddenly aware that the room has got dark.
GRAHAM *switches a lamp on then sits back down.*

(*Topping up* RICHARD's *glass.*) Here.

RICHARD. Um, thanks.

Pause.

GRAHAM. You don't like Plymouth very much, do you, Richard?

RICHARD. Not really.

Beat.

I think – I think it's shit.

GRAHAM *laughs.*

Excuse my language but – I really think it is. It's completely shit.

GRAHAM. Oh, it's not that bad. I haven't seen much of it yet but the Barbican's quite nice and – you have the ocean.

RICHARD. I think it's crap. There's nothing, like – nothing ever happens here – nothing interesting or amazing or – or even anything [horrible]. And most of the people are – like, when they walk, they can barely lift their feet off the ground. I mean, they all walk round like they're kind-of monged-out most of the time. Haven't you seen that?

GRAHAM. No, I can't say I have.

RICHARD. Well, they do. And it's so – I mean – this town, it's so small. It's, like, *miniscule* – it doesn't even have a Pizza Express.

GRAHAM *laughs and shifts into a more comfortable position in his chair.*

(*Warming to his theme.*) Because – because I mean, how can you live all your life somewhere that doesn't have a Pizza Express? Everyone who lives here, they think it's the centre of the… But it's so… Because if they bombed it tomorrow, if they put a great big nuclear bomb under, like, Debenhams and it flattened the whole thing then the rest of the world would be very sad and they'd miss it for a few days and everything but would it – I mean, the world would go on, wouldn't it? It wouldn't be like the world couldn't function any more without the people living in this town. There would be no possibility of the world stopping or – or anything really changing. And after a while, all the people in this town and all the things they'd done, they'd just be, like, memories in other people's heads. And then, the people that had the memories would die and then they'd just be some people in photographs who nobody knows. Does that make sense?

GRAHAM. I think so. (*Beat.*) So where would you like to be instead?

RICHARD. I want to go to London. I'm going to go to London. I want to study there. Art.

GRAHAM. You want to be an artist?

Beat.

RICHARD. I do, yes. (*Beat.*) I haven't told anyone that before.

GRAHAM. Well, I'm honoured. And you're going to London?

RICHARD. Yes. I mean, I want to. There's this college there, Goldsmiths, do you know it?

GRAHAM. Oh yes.

RICHARD. And – I don't know if I'm good enough but – to get in there – but Mr Hendricks – he's my art teacher – he says I might be. He says he thinks I've got a chance.

GRAHAM. I'm sure you have.

RICHARD. My parents, they think I should do law at, um, Reading or something.

GRAHAM. I see.

RICHARD. I think – I think they'll be sort-of – sort-of devastated when I tell them.

GRAHAM. Will they?

RICHARD. Yes. Actually I think Dad is going to throw a total shitfit but – but I think my mum will understand. And there's no way I'm going there so…

GRAHAM. Because you're going to Goldsmiths.

RICHARD. Yes.

RICHARD *smiles, as if a weight has been lifted.*

GRAHAM. Well, Richard, I say go for it. In my experience, most people are too afraid to do what they really want. You have to seize each moment. That's the key, Richard – don't ever look back. Just this moment. Do you understand?

They sit there for a few moments. GRAHAM *drinks more of his wine.*

Penny?

RICHARD *doesn't understand this.*

What are you thinking about?

RICHARD. Oh. I was thinking about this girl, Claire Dunlop.

GRAHAM. Is that your girlfriend?

RICHARD *laughs nervously at this idea.*

What?

RICHARD. Nothing, it's just… She was this girl. She was in Year 11 when I was in Year 9.

GRAHAM. Right.

RICHARD. I was thinking about when she won this competition. To meet Westlife. All the other girls in Year 11 were so jealous that they stopped talking to her and they spread it round that she had, like, Aids or something. And they drove her to London in this, like, incredibly stupid stretch limo. And they put her in this posh hotel, not The Ritz but like The Ritz, and then she went to the concert and then halfway through the concert, one of Westlife, like Bryan or Paddy or whatever, gets her on stage and sings to her and hands her a red rose. And then – and then they drive her back here in the stretch limo. And that's it. And then two weeks later, they find her in the girls' toilets behind the science block. She'd slit her wrists.

GRAHAM. Jesus.

RICHARD. Oh, she didn't die. But then she did her GSCEs and she gets like a D and an E or something and has to leave school and she gets a job in the Ginsters factory making pasties out of, like, pig's eyelids – and I was sort-of thinking that her life is pretty shitty, isn't it – but I bet meeting Westlife didn't help. I bet she knew that nothing in her life would ever be as good as being handed a rose by Bryan from Westlife. I bet that afterwards, knowing that the absolute best moment of her life had already happened made everything –

made everything seem approximately fifty per cent more rubbish in comparison, don't you – don't you think?

GRAHAM. Yes, quite possibly. (*Beat.*) Who are Westlife?

RICHARD. It's a band. A boyband.

GRAHAM. Ah.

Pause.

(*Leaning forward.*) Richard, have you ever seen Mapplethorpe?

RICHARD. Um.

GRAHAM. Robert Mapplethorpe. He's a photographer.

RICHARD. I think – I think I've heard of him. (*He hasn't.*)

GRAHAM. Oh. Well, you would really – I think you would really like his work. It's —

GRAHAM *gets up.*

It's very interesting. Mapplethorpe lived in New York in the 1970s and '80s and – he was very much an outsider like you but he created these images that – here we are.

GRAHAM *finds the book,* Altars *by Robert Mapplethorpe, straight away and brings it over to* RICHARD. *For the first time, he sits down next to* RICHARD *on the sofa – there's an intimacy that wasn't there before.* GRAHAM *starts flicking through the book, making comments on selected images. We don't actually see the images that* GRAHAM *is talking about but, at a certain point, something in* RICHARD's *response – perhaps in his breathing – suggests a shift in the kind of images he is viewing.*

So he's very much working within the great tradition of black-and-white portraiture a bit like Avedon. Very simple set-ups and a very instinctive, very potent use of light and shadow...

Pause.

I mean, something like that, it's very simple but the sense of texture is – well, it's tremendous...

Pause.

He was very much drawn to religious iconography so he incorporates all these bold geometric shapes and the pictures almost become like – like altarpieces, do you see that?

RICHARD. Yes.

GRAHAM. And the composition can be very formal, very thought-through but then – yes – here, he's going for something far more, um, spontaneous.

Beat.

That's interesting, isn't it?

RICHARD. –

GRAHAM. Is that something you've thought about, Richard?

RICHARD. –

GRAHAM. Is that something you'd like to do?

RICHARD. –

GRAHAM *continues flicking through the book as if nothing has happened.*

GRAHAM. Ah, now this one. This one is where he switched from Polaroid to a Hasselblad medium format. It doesn't seem like a big difference but there's a – there's a kind of crispness to the lighting that really elevates everything.

Pause.

And here, he's taking elements of – of constructivist collage to disrupt the formality of the subject. Do you see that? (*Beat.*) Do you see that, Richard?

Beat.

RICHARD. Yes. I think so.

GRAHAM *suddenly stops flicking the pages.*

GRAHAM. You've got so much potential, Richard. You know that, don't you?

RICHARD *doesn't know how to respond to this. After a brief pause,* GRAHAM *continues flicking through the pages of the book for several moments.*

Sudden fade.

Two

*September, 2005. The same room. It's mid-morning and the
room is filled with sunlight. There's no furniture in the room and
it's clearly been empty for some time. In the middle of the living
room stand* BECCI *and* LAURA.

Both BECCI *and* LAURA *are heavily pregnant.*

LAURA *is looking intently at the house.* BECCI *is looking
intently at* LAURA.

LAURA. Do you think it's floorboards? (*Springs lightly up and
down on the floor.*) It would be floorboards, wouldn't it?

   Pause.

   Love the coving. Or is it cornicing? Never really know the…
   (*Looks at* BECCI.) What? (*Beat.*) Have I got [something]?

   Beat.

   (*Not unkindly.*) What is it?

BECCI. Laura Prowse.

LAURA. Oh. Right.

   Beat.

BECCI. Prowsey.

   A polite laugh from LAURA.

   Prowse the Mouse.

LAURA (*quietly*). Never really liked that one.

BECCI. God. (*Beat.*) And you've got boobs.

   Another polite laugh.

   (*Laughing.*) You never had friggin' boobs.

LAURA. Well. I am [pregnant] so…

   Beat.

BECCI. Can I have a touch?

LAURA. Of my – breasts?

BECCI. Eww, no, lezza. That – (*Indicates bump.*)

LAURA. Oh. Right. Um. (*Beat.*) Okay.

    LAURA *submits to* BECCI *placing her hands on her stomach.*

BECCI. Fuck me. And how many months?

LAURA. Er, almost seven.

BECCI. So weird. I mean *good weird*, but… oh, guess who else's in the club?

LAURA. Um.

BECCI. Guess.

LAURA. I really don't –

BECCI. Dawn Bennett's sister.

LAURA. Oh.

BECCI. Right old fatty-bum-bum she is, not that she was ever anorexic.

LAURA. Right.

BECCI. Keeps making up all these cravings, Dawn says. 'Baby wants a Double Sausage and Egg McMuffin.' 'Baby made me eat a whole Chocolate Orange.' (*Laughs.*)

LAURA (*laughs*). Right (*Beat.*) Becci, I've just got a few –

BECCI (*a thought*). Hey! Just a sec.

LAURA. Oh, sure.

    BECCI *gets her phone out of her bag. Rings a number.*

BECCI (*into the phone*). Wotcha, babes.

    Beat.

    Yeah, same to you. Listen –

    Beat. LAURA *gets out her phone and starts checking texts, etc.*

Yeah, I know. Listen – so I turn up for an appointment at that house today –

Beat.

That house. Nine New Park Road.

Beat.

(*Quieter.*) Yeah, I know it's… (*Looking round nervously.*) Fucking Phil, I said to him I wouldn't…

Beat.

Yeah, I know but. (*Bit louder.*) But – listen, guess – guess who I'm showing around, Chantelle?

LAURA (*looks up from phone*). Oh. (*Smiles a little too politely.*)

BECCI. Go on, Chantelle, guess.

Beat.

No. Why would it be [him]?

Beat.

(*Filthy laugh.*) Oh, well, no. (*Beat.*) Laura Prowse!

Beat.

I'm not shitting you, Chantelle. Laura friggin' Prowse.

LAURA. Actually it's Higgins now but –

BECCI (*to Chantelle*). I know!

Beat.

Says she's had enough of that London. (*Winks at* LAURA.)

LAURA. I didn't say that…

Beat.

BECCI. Says she's moving back down.

LAURA. That's not really –

BECCI (*to Chantelle*). I know! (*Beat.*) Yeah to Plymouth.

Beat.

(*To* LAURA.) Chantelle says about-friggin'-time. (*To Chantelle*.) And hey, guess what. She's only having a baby.

Beat.

I know! She's got tits now and everything.

Beat.

(*Laughs*.) Yeah, I know. They're, like – massive.

Beat.

(*Laughs*.) I know.

Beat.

LAURA. It's just that my train's in, like –

BECCI (*to Chantelle, laughing*). You slag. (*To* LAURA.) Chantelle says she wants to join our gang. Says she's gonna go down Union Street tonight and get inseminated by some nineteen-year-old lad so she doesn't feel left out.

Beat.

She says she's only joking.

Mouths 'she's not'.

(*To Chantelle*.) What? I didn't say /

Beat.

Here, she wants to say hello.

BECCI *tries to give the phone to* LAURA.

LAURA. Oh. Um, no, I'd rather –

BECCI. Go on.

LAURA. No, I'd really – I mean – I'm okay.

BECCI. Go on.

LAURA. Er, no. No, thank you.

Pause.

BECCI. Um, Chantelle. No, it's me. No, she doesn't – think she's feeling a little bit – shy. Yeah. (*Beat*.) Down on the train this morning. (*Beat*.) Yeah. (*Beat*.) Alright then, well,

I better go. Yeah. Alright. (*Beat*.) I'll See *You* Next Tuesday, slag. Bye.

Beat.

LAURA. I'm sorry, I just –

BECCI. No no, it's –

LAURA. Felt a bit on the spot there.

BECCI. S'only Chantelle but.

LAURA. Just felt a bit weird to /

BECCI. Yeah, no.

LAURA. Wasn't really prepared so.

BECCI. Yeah, no worries.

Pause.

LAURA. So… (*Jokily*.) back to the house.

BECCI. Right. The house. Okay. (*More professional but with a distinct unease*.) Lovely. So, you've – you've seen all the rooms now. Had a little nosey.

LAURA (*jokily*). By myself.

BECCI. By yourself, yes, sorry about that, and um – so this is the lounge. Obviously. And, um – any questions about the house before we…

LAURA. Um. No, I mean it all seems very /

BECCI. Good, okay. (*Beat*.) Well, let's…

BECCI *is trying to leave,* LAURA *is not*.

LAURA. Just trying to – visualise how everything will…

BECCI. Oh okay.

LAURA. Have this picture in my head of how I… Done moodboards and…

BECCI. Right okay.

LAURA. Sort of, sort of 'seaside chic but with a modern twist'. (*Sheepish laugh*.)

BECCI. Oh.

LAURA. Kind of vintage-y I guess but not too – retro or...

BECCI. Yeah /

LAURA. So have, sort of touches of colour in the bedrooms and the nursery but then make it more – more cool and neutral down here, perhaps. (*Of the lounge*.) I mean, maybe it could take something darker actually – maybe Downpipe or Pigeon or – cosy it up a little bit.

BECCI. Yeah, Laura, you did /

LAURA. Or – God – you could totally just, like, knock it through – straight through to the kitchen. (*Starts to get carried away, moving around the room*.) You'd be able to see right through to the garden from here – yeah, really bring the outside in. And we could have the dining table that Mark said we'd never have room for and then have, y'know, like bi-folding doors or. And a massive light fitting here. God, yeah... And shelves! (*Gestures around the fireplace – rapt*.) And our rugs! (*To* BECCI.) We can't even have them all out in the London flat – there isn't room!

BECCI. Laura, you did speak to someone in the office, didn't you?

LAURA. Sorry?

BECCI. About – about the house, I mean.

LAURA (*distracted*). Oh. Yes. (*Beat*.) But maybe you wouldn't want to knock it through. Maybe it's actually quite nice to have separate... Because – what would it be in here?

BECCI. What?

LAURA. In here. (*Beat*.) The size, Becci.

BECCI. Oh, um. I don't know.

LAURA. Um, what about the sheet?

BECCI. Right, yes, the sheet. (*Starts looking through the bag*.) I don't normally do this one so.

LAURA. You said.

BECCI (*rifling through bag*). Normally it's Phil who does Nine New Park Road but he's on a stag thing in Kraków and then it's Neil but he's off with the shits so – here we go. Oop no, that's Thornley Street. Think you'll really like Thornley Street. Ex-local but very good spec. On at the same price but… Here we are. Lounge. Oh it doesn't say.

LAURA. Oh.

BECCI. Sorry. Bit old these details.

LAURA. Right.

BECCI. Need a bit of updating.

LAURA. Sure.

BECCI (*looking round with distaste*). First time we've shown the place in, like, forever so.

LAURA. Sure. Well, let's just – tape measure – (*Starts looking through her bag.*)

BECCI (*uneasy*). Oh.

LAURA. If that's alright.

BECCI. No, yeah, course. (*Beat.*) I mean, we've probably got it back at the office but –

LAURA. Just take a [sec].

BECCI. Um, okay. (*Beat.*)

LAURA. Could you just – hold that, please?

BECCI. Er.

They move around the room at LAURA*'s prompting.* BECCI *holds the other end of the tape measure.* LAURA *has a little notebook into which she draws a plan of the room and adds each measurement in turn.* BECCI *nervously makes conversation.* LAURA *is distracted by the task in hand.*

God, can't believe we're both….

LAURA. Yeah.

BECCI. I mean, what are the chances?

LAURA. Yeah.

Beat.

BECCI. Hey, now we can do stuff together!

LAURA. Uh-huh.

BECCI. Like, baby things.

LAURA (*neutral*). Yeah.

BECCI. Go round each other's houses and – take the kiddies to the park.

LAURA. Mm.

BECCI. Be such a laugh.

LAURA. Yeah.

BECCI. Pick up where we /

LAURA. Right, sure.

BECCI (*a thought*). Oh my God, we should do baby yoga!

LAURA. Oh, right.

BECCI. We have that in Plymouth now.

LAURA. Uh-huh.

BECCI (*laughs*). 'Why d'you want a baby who can put its' /

LAURA. Right yeah.

BECCI. 'Put its leg behind its head.'

LAURA (*distracted*). Yeah.

BECCI. That's what Jamie says but /

LAURA. Jamie?

BECCI. Oh.

LAURA. Jamie… Jamie.

BECCI. Yeah.

LAURA. Oh right. (*Beat.*) And he's the [father]?

BECCI. Yeah.

Beat.

LAURA. Wow, that's – wow. (*Beat*.) Congratulations!

BECCI. (*awkward*) Thanks.

Pause.

LAURA. Right. So that's – what's that? That's twelve by fourteen foot. And that's – (*Tots it up with the calculator on her phone.*) wow, that's – yeah. (*Beat*.)

LAURA stops what she's doing and takes the room in.

I mean, I never thought we could… A – a place like [this].

Pause.

BECCI (*wanting to leave*). Okay super. Are we all done?

LAURA. Um.

BECCI. Because I'm just going to whizz you over to Thornley Street, Laura. Think you'll really like Thornley Street.

LAURA. Actually /

BECCI. Owner's just put in new PVC and /

LAURA. Actually, Becci, I'm not quite done here. If that's…

BECCI. Oh. Okay.

LAURA (*gets camera out*). Can I just?

BECCI. Yeah. No. Sure sure. (*Beat*.) I mean, there's pictures on the sheet but – no, course.

LAURA starts moving around the room, taking photographs.

All the girls round here, they pierce their babies' ears.

LAURA (*appalled*). Oh I know.

BECCI. So I'm gonna pierce its nose.

LAURA. Oh. Right.

BECCI. Something – something different, isn't it?

LAURA. Yes. Yes it is.

Perhaps BECCI has picked up on the neutrality of LAURA's answer. Pause.

BECCI (*brightly*). So. Who's the lucky fella?

LAURA. Sorry?

BECCI. I mean, who – (*Points at her belly.*)

LAURA. Oh. Yes. (*Laughs.*) That'll be Mark, my husband. (*Beat.*) I think.

BECCI. You're not sure?

LAURA. No, I – I am, Becci. That was a joke.

BECCI. Oh right. Ha! And what does Mark?

LAURA. He's – an academic. A, er, marine biologist.

BECCI. Is he, wow!

LAURA. He's just got a post at the university. That's why we've…

BECCI. Ah okay. Why you're moving back.

LAURA. Um, not really –

BECCI. Sorry?

LAURA. Not really – calling it that actually.

BECCI. What?

LAURA. 'Moving back.'

BECCI. Oh.

LAURA. I mean, I guess it's – maybe *technically* but – but it's not really… *like* [that].

BECCI. Okay.

LAURA. Because – because I mean, Plymouth's changed so much since I was…

BECCI. Has it?

LAURA. Yes. I barely recognise it, to be honest! What with all the – all the shops and the – the cafés and –

BECCI. Cafés?

LAURA. And what have you. (*Beat.*) And there's the theatre and –

BECCI. Very good pantos…

LAURA. And there just seems to be a real – a real buzz about the place. Right now.

BECCI. Does there?

LAURA. Yes. Yes, I think so.

BECCI. Oh. Okay.

LAURA. So… yeah. (*Beat.*) Just gonna – text some pics to Mark if that's /

BECCI. Yeah, sure.

> *Pause.*

> Did you not like London then or?

LAURA. No, London's – I mean, it's so dirty and obviously it takes, like, *a year* to get anywhere but – London's great. It's – yeah. It's just Mark – for his career…

BECCI. Ah, is it not [going well]?

LAURA. No, no, I mean, his career's going really well at the moment. Done some quite groundbreaking – had some quite important papers published on the – on the annual migration patterns of, um, dogfish.

BECCI. Dogfish?

LAURA. Yes. It's quite a – quite a *vital* area of research actually but, it's – well, it's very valuable in terms of scientific progress but, er, where we live – er, Hackney?

BECCI. Oh right.

LAURA. Well, it's East London but there *are* some really nice bits but – um, yeah, where we live… I guess there's not so much… There's not much call for someone with a PhD in Marine Conservation. In Hackney.

BECCI. Is there not?

LAURA. No, not really. And I mean, the rents have sort-of – sort of rocketed in the past few [years]. And since they, um, they *restructured* my job then –

BECCI. Oh.

LAURA. And it's all done on income multiples now, isn't it? And I mean, you never – you never *picture yourself* living in a small one-bedroom flat in Hackney when you're nearly thirty, do you? You imagine this, well, a big house or – just something...

BECCI. Okay.

LAURA. So really, it's just – it's just not a *logical* thing to – live there.

BECCI. Oh.

LAURA. Any more.

BECCI. Oh.

LAURA. Yeah.

BECCI. That's a shame.

LAURA. Um, no, Becci. That's not [what I'm saying]. Because it's – it's really quite a positive thing, actually.

BECCI. Is it?

LAURA. Yes. Yes, it is.

BECCI. Okay.

LAURA. Because, well, Mark's got this job and – and he's always wanted to live by the sea so... And we can live with my mother while we're doing somewhere up – which she's *totally* fine with so – and...

BECCI. That's great.

LAURA. So it's really – it's very much a – a new adventure for us. For both of us. Really.

BECCI. Fantastic.

LAURA. It's just – it's just a brilliant opportunity to build a new life.

BECCI. In Plymouth.

LAURA. Yes. (*Beat.*) In Plymouth.

Pause.

BECCI (*trying to get her out the door*). Okay, lovely, all done? So. Thornley Street. Here's the deets. Think you're gonna love Thornley Street.

LAURA. Thanks. Um, Becci, can I just ask about /

BECCI. Sure sure.

LAURA. The floor.

BECCI. Right.

LAURA. Because wood floors are sort of – pivotal to the whole um…

BECCI. Okay.

LAURA. So I really would like to know if it's [floorboards] underneath.

BECCI. Okay. Um. I mean, I can check with the office when I get back and /

LAURA. Yeah. (*Beat.*) Couldn't we just – a corner or something?

BECCI. Oh. Um.

LAURA. I know you do that sometimes but /

BECCI. Yeah, no, it's not /

LAURA. I mean, no one's living here and…

BECCI. It's just – the clients sometimes /

LAURA. And we can put it back again so…

BECCI. Yeah, I really don't think it's /

LAURA. It would just be very – helpful. For me, Becci. You know?

BECCI. Um…

LAURA (*seeing her chance*). Okay, I'll be quick.

BECCI. Um…

LAURA *finds a corner of the carpet, lowers herself down and tries to pull it loose.* BECCI *watches with growing unease.*

Laura…

LAURA (*pulling at the carpet*). Can't seem to /

BECCI. Laura, someone did talk to you – they definitely did talk to you about the house, didn't they?

LAURA. Can't seem to get a handle on it.

BECCI. Because we have a kind of – obligation – when anything's – when anyone's – y'know, *died* – in one of the houses.

LAURA. Ah, now that's /

BECCI. And I mean, you're one of my – one of my oldest friends so I wouldn't want to…

LAURA. Give it a bit of [welly].

BECCI. Laura, could you stop that for a moment, please.

LAURA (*to the carpet*). Come on!

BECCI. Laura, please just –

LAURA. Think I've –

BECCI. Just stop it, Laura. Stop it!

LAURA. Yes!

The carpet suddenly comes loose. There's dust and LAURA *topples backwards slightly.*

Oh.

BECCI. Oh shit.

LAURA. Ouf.

BECCI. Shit, are you –

LAURA. Yeah, I'm /

BECCI. Are you okay?

LAURA. I'm fine, Becci. Just a little /

BECCI. Oh God.

LAURA. Just winded myself a little bit.

BECCI. Oh God.

LAURA. Be fine if I just – sit here for a moment.

BECCI. Are you?

LAURA. Yes, I'm /

BECCI. Should I phone someone or –

LAURA. No, it's – really.

BECCI. Oh.

LAURA. It's okay. Really.

Pause while LAURA *catches her breath.*

BECCI. I told Phil I wouldn't do this house.

LAURA. Becci…

BECCI. I told Phil that. It's not – right.

LAURA. What?

BECCI. I'm sorry, Laura. I was trying to tell you.

LAURA. Tell me what?

BECCI. It's – this house. It's just…

LAURA. Becci, what are you /

BECCI. Used to walk past it on my way to Chantelle's and you could just – you could just feel the…

LAURA. What are you talking about?

BECCI. Phil always getting me to do this one but I never would. I never would, you know.

LAURA. Becci, I'm fine now.

BECCI. Can't you feel it?

LAURA. I'm fine now, honestly.

BECCI. Can't you feel it, Laura? It's like…

Beat.

LAURA. I don't know what you're talking about, Becci.

A pause.

Becci.

BECCI. Yes.

LAURA. Can you help me up, please?

BECCI. Oh shit, course.

BECCI helps LAURA up.

LAURA. Thank you.

BECCI (*back to professional Becci*). Okay. Super. So let's just –
yeah – let's just go now and. (*Sees LAURA moving towards
the pulled-away carpet.*) Oh leave that.

They collect their things together. LAURA gets a text.

LAURA. Oh, it's just Mark.

LAURA laughs at something in the text.

BECCI. Is it /

LAURA. No, it's [nothing].

BECCI. What?

LAURA. Oh, it's just…

BECCI. What?

LAURA. We have this friend Luke who – he's a graphic
designer but he also does these parties and /

BECCI. Oh right.

LAURA. And silly but… we all get together, like, once a month
for dinner. Kind of like an unofficial *supper-club*-type thing
and – and we always find, like, the weirdest restaurants and
we'll go and dress up in, in the traditional costumes of the
food so.

BECCI. Oh.

LAURA. Like if we're going to a Spanish restaurant then we'll
all dress in, like, sombreros or… And – (*Laughs.*) Mark's
just – on the internet he's found this place in, like, West
Norwood that serves *elk meat* /

BECCI. Elk meat?

LAURA. He says we should all go there and dress up as, like,
Eskimos in fur coats and… Such an idiot.

Beat.

BECCI. Eskimos?

LAURA (*embarrassed*). Yeah, it's like a – like a fancy-dress thing.

BECCI. Oh.

LAURA. Sort of silly but – because that's what we do so…

BECCI. Oh okay.

LAURA. Just gonna – text him [back].

LAURA *moves away slightly and starts texting. A pause.*

BECCI. Hey, they've got this new night at Flares now.

LAURA. Oh right.

BECCI. 'School Daze'. But like, daze is spelt d–a–z–e not d–a… yeah. And everyone goes in, like, pigtails and school ties and. Only it's not kids, it's people our age and.

LAURA. Right, yeah.

BECCI. Hey, we should go some time. You, me, Chantelle and – and Jamie and. Be a right giggle. Try and squeeze into our old uniforms, yeah?

LAURA. –

BECCI. Hey, Laura, what's your number and I'll put it in my phone.

LAURA *continues to text* MARK *back.*

Then I'll send you a text and you'll have mine so.

LAURA. –

BECCI. Or – or I could just give you my number, if it's… Laura?

Beat.

LAURA. No.

Beat.

There's no point.

BECCI. Oh.

LAURA. I'm – I'm not going to call you, Becci.

Beat.

BECCI. Oh.

Beat.

LAURA (*looks up from texting*). I'm sorry, I'm not trying to be cruel, it's just /

BECCI. Oh.

LAURA. I'm just – being realistic. I'm sorry.

Pause.

BECCI. I don't really [understand]. Because you're one of my – one of my oldest friends. And you're moving back here so /

LAURA (*politely frustrated*). But that's not – I'm not 'moving back', Becci.

BECCI. Oh.

LAURA. That's not what I'm doing.

BECCI. Then –

LAURA. It's – it has to be something new. This. Do you see? I have to keep… Forward momentum.

BECCI. Right.

LAURA. A new start.

BECCI. Right.

LAURA. Do you understand?

Pause.

BECCI. I just thought it would be nice to…

LAURA. No. (*Beat.*) Sorry.

Pause.

BECCI (*shaking slightly but back into professional Becci*). Okay, lovely. So we've got all your details on our database now and – and if any future properties match your particular specifications, then we'll – we'll be in touch. (*Collecting her things together.*) Lovely. So it was great to see you again, Laura, and have a safe journey back. Here, that's yours.

LAURA. Um, Becci.

BECCI. Yes.

LAURA. Could you ask Phil to call me when he's back please.

BECCI. Yeah, course. (*Beat.*) It's not – you're not gonna say anything about today, are you?

LAURA. Sorry?

BECCI. Because – because the carpet was sort of your idea so –

LAURA. Becci, it's not… (*Beat.*) I'd like to make an offer. On the house.

Pause.

BECCI. Sorry, I don't – I don't understand. (*Beat.*) This house.

LAURA. Yes.

BECCI. You want to – you want to make an offer on Nine New Park Road?

LAURA. Yes.

Beat.

BECCI. No. No. (*Beat.*) I won't /

LAURA. Well, it's really not your call, Becci, so.

BECCI. This – and you want to /

LAURA (*making to leave*). Can you just ask Phil to /

BECCI. You want to live in it? You're going to bring your baby into it? Nope, sorry but…

LAURA. Just ask Phil to call me, Becci, okay?

Beat.

BECCI. Are you mad though, Laura?

LAURA. I wouldn't expect you to –

BECCI. Are you actually just, like, mad?

LAURA. Wouldn't expect you to get it.

BECCI. What? Get fucking what?

Beat.

LAURA. Do you know where I live right now? Do you though? Me and my husband live in a space, um, basically the size of this room, no actually probably smaller than… and now there's a baby and – and it's not like we're stupid or – or lazy or – trying to get something for free. We've worked hard, we've worked *really fucking hard* and. Do you think I could ever – ever afford to buy this house if someone hadn't…

BECCI. But someone died here. A boy died here, Laura.

LAURA. That's /

BECCI. A boy was *killed* here and you /

LAURA. That's… unfortunate but.

BECCI. Unfortunate! It's more than fucking unfortunate, Laura! It's really *gross* and just, just *tragic* and…

LAURA. But that's nothing to do with me. That's – don't you see? It's nothing to do with my life. It doesn't – it doesn't *register*.

BECCI. What are you talking about?

LAURA. You think this is the first house that something like that's happened in? You think every house you show people round doesn't have some kind of awful… because they do, Becci. All of them. Death and sadness and… But that's just – history. That's – it's done with.

BECCI. God, that is so like you. A boy was /

LAURA. And you think, what, that he's still – what?

BECCI. Always so, like – cold and…

LAURA. Still lurking around the hallways, Becci? Still rattling his chains?

BECCI. That's sick –

LAURA. No, it's not. It's really not. What's – what's sick is clinging on to the past like some bloody… As if this house is *infected* or. Because it's not. It's just some walls and some windows and… It's just a house, Becci. It's a house with good period features that I can buy and make nice and raise a family in. And everything that's happened, it's all just – it's gone.

Pause.

BECCI. Well, I'm not gonna let you.

LAURA. What?

BECCI. I'm not gonna let you.

LAURA. Becky, this is /

BECCI. Not gonna let you buy it.

LAURA. This is stupid.

BECCI. Yeah, that's right. Stupid Becci.

LAURA. That's not /

BECCI. Stupid Becci from Swilly...

LAURA. I never said [that].

BECCI (*losing her breath*). You – you think you can just turn up one day. You think you can swan back from London and buy some – some famous fucking paedo house and make it /

LAURA. Shut up, Becci.

BECCI (*breathing hard*). You think because you're Laura Prowse you can – what? – make it into your dream home, your 'Forever House'.

LAURA (*concerned*). Becci...

BECCI. Oh that's right, I forgot. Laura Prowse does what she likes. Laura Prowse's shit don't stink like the... like...

LAURA. Becci, are you?

BECCI. Yeah, I'm /

LAURA. You're really pale.

BECCI. No, it's –

LAURA. Shit.

BECCI. Just – just think I need to sit down.

LAURA (*look round*). Okay. Okay.

BECCI. Be alright if I... where's a chair?

LAURA. Chair chair... Um, think I saw some in the kitchen.

BECCI. No, don't [go].

LAURA. It's fine, just...

BECCI. Please don't /

> LAURA *leaves. For several moments,* BECCI *is standing by herself. She is trying to control her breathing but feels the room pressing in.* LAURA *comes back with two chairs.*

LAURA. Here we go.

> BECCI *doesn't really want to touch the chair.*

Becci, you need to sit down. (*Beat.*) It's just a bloody chair.

> BECCI *sits. After a moment,* LAURA *sits too. Long pause.*

Are you sure you're [alright]?

> BECCI *nods. Another pause as* BECCI *tries to get her breath back. Eventually:*

BECCI. Is this...

LAURA. What?

BECCI. Is this – because of Jamie?

LAURA. Becci...

BECCI. Because we didn't – when you were... It was much later.

LAURA. I know.

BECCI. And Jamie said it was you that didn't want the – not him...

LAURA (*laughing at the sad absurdness of the idea*). It's not about Jamie Price.

> *Long pause.*

BECCI. He was fifteen or sixteen.

LAURA. Jamie was /

BECCI. Not Jamie, the lad who died here. He was fifteen or sixteen.

LAURA. Becci…

BECCI. He was in the same year as my cousin Amy.

LAURA. I don't really want to hear this.

LAURA *gets her things together.*

BECCI. She said he was /

LAURA. I'm not listening to this, Becci.

LAURA *stands up and heads to the door. At some point during the next bit, she stops.*

BECCI. She said he was always taking pictures of people when he thought they weren't looking. She said most people thought he was a bit of a freak but I said you shouldn't speak ill of the dead. She said oh no she wasn't, she said that he didn't have many friends but that she'd always thought he was quite nice. Said there was one time when they'd all gone on a school trip to see the birds at Slapton Ley and she'd fallen out with Kerry Bonser and Danielle Heybridge and there'd been no more seats on the bus on the way back and she ended up sat next to him and she hadn't wanted to talk to him at first on account of him being a bit of a freak but then he offered her a bite of his peanut Boost and she'd never had a peanut Boost before and everyone was saying how shit the trip was and, like, how boring the birds were but he said he thought it was actually quite interesting. And she said she thought it was too. And then it was a few weeks later and she found this photograph slipped into her locker and it was a photograph of this, like, bird, that they'd seen at Slapton and she knew it was from him and she said it was, like, the most lovely picture she'd ever seen. And she took it home and she stuck it by her bed and she – she always meant to, um, mention it to him but she never did. And then – they weren't in the same class or anything – and then every time she saw him in the corridor, she'd, like, turn the other way because she was a bit embarrassed about it but she didn't know why. And then she never talked to him again after that.

A long pause.

Jamie always said /

LAURA. What?

BECCI. Jamie said you wouldn't have made a good mother anyway.

Another pause.

LAURA. What colour do you think. For in here?

BECCI *shakes her head.*

I was thinking about – it's this shade called Cornforth White.

Beat.

It's a sort of – sort of whitey colour but with subtle hints of grey and brown.

Beat.

And then upstairs – upstairs, I was going to go a bit more – be a bit more daring maybe?

Beat.

And then in the nursery, I was going to go for – it's this pale blue called Borrowed Light.

Longer beat.

They say you should have fun with colour.

BECCI (*neutral*). Do they?

LAURA. Yes. Yes, they do.

Sudden fade.

Three

May 2012. The same room. It's gone midnight – dark except for one or two lamps. There's a different sofa and armchair and a very domestic feeling to the space. Boxes and piles of stuff once again litter the room, perhaps including a few toys, but this time things are being packed up.

LUCY is standing in the centre of the room, deep in thought.

MARK is stood just inside the door with two cans of beer.

MARK is dressed in work shirt, tie and trousers – smart on this morning but now looking rather crumpled.

MARK. It's original.

LUCY. What?

MARK. The cornicing.

LUCY. –

MARK. You seem interested in it. The cornicing.

LUCY. Do I?

MARK. Uh-huh.

LUCY. It's very – ornate.

MARK. Yes. One of the things we liked.

LUCY. We?

A pause.

MARK (*pop quiz*). Coving and cornicing. What's the difference?

    LUCY *shrugs*.

    Coving's the boring flat bit that runs across the room and cornicing's all the – all the fiddly doo-dahs. Scrolls and whatnot.

LUCY (*not especially interested*). Ah.

MARK. A lot of people think they're the same thing but they're – they're not so – so there you go.

A small pause.

Ever done the quiz?

LUCY *looks at him.*

Sunday nights. Barman with the ginger beard wears a top hat. Takes it very seriously.

LUCY. Sounds fun.

MARK. Is actually. Gets quite a big crowd. For The Fortescue.

LUCY. Seven or eight people then?

MARK (*playing along*). Ooh, at least... We won twenty pounds once.

LUCY. We?

MARK *looks at* LUCY. LUCY *starts moving around the room, inspecting its contents.* MARK *is looking for some music to put on.*

I don't think I've ever won anything in my life. I mean, everyone always says that, don't they?

MARK. Do they?

LUCY. Yeah. Like, you're watching the Oscars and there's Scarlett Johansson or some dickhead and they're like 'ooh, I never win anything, me' and you're like 'fuck off, Scarlett, you twat'. But I've honestly never won a thing.

MARK. Never?

LUCY. Uh-uh. Not a sausage.

Beat.

MARK. Not a sausage?

LUCY. No.

MARK. Not even one little sausage.

LUCY (*not unfriendly*). Dickhead.

Pause.

MARK. Did you know that the first commercially available prophylactic sheath was actually created by a sausage-maker?

She gives him a look.

They used lamb cecum, which is the – well, it's the blind pouch connecting the ileum with the ascending colon of the largest intestine and /

LUCY. Is this what you do?

MARK. What?

LUCY. When you're drunk? Talk about sausage casings.

MARK. –

LUCY. I was shagging this boy once and every time he got drunk he'd always start talking about Radiohead.

MARK. Right.

LUCY. Like, I think he secretly wanted to nosh off Thom Yorke or something, y'know?

MARK. Okay.

LUCY. So maybe sausage casings are, like, your Thom Yorke?

MARK. Maybe sausage casings are, like, my Thom Yorke?

LUCY. Yeah.

Again, he can't think of a good reply.

Or – (*Turning just a little bit nasty.*) maybe you think that segueing from sausages to condoms via some geeky trivia about lambs' intestines is sort of – sort of sexy and clever? Maybe this is your idea of foreplay.

MARK. Crap idea of foreplay if it is.

LUCY. I agree. Pretty rusty at this, aren't we, Mark?

Beat. She is flicking through his books, running her fingers over the spines.

(*Selecting* Captain Corelli's Mandolin.) Have you read this?

MARK. No, I don't think so.

LUCY. Don't bother, it's shit.

Beat.

Where are all the textbooks?

MARK. Sorry?

LUCY. The textbooks. From when you went to university.

MARK. –

LUCY. Whenever you go round to someone's flat – or house or
whatever – and you look at their bookcase, they've always
got, like, all their textbooks from university lined up on
display. Even though they left university, like, *years* ago.

MARK. Ah.

LUCY. And it's like – it's like they think you're gonna be *really*
impressed by the fact that once, a very very long time ago,
they read a textbook. Because they had to.

MARK. Ha.

LUCY. And of course, you just know they've lugged them from
poxy flat to poxy flat, like some kind of – some *talisman* of
intelligence, even though – even though they probably only,
y'know, skim-read a chapter or, like, read the introduction.

MARK *smiles at this.*

So where are yours?

MARK. My textbooks?

LUCY. Yeah.

MARK. Um, my textbooks are in my office. At the university.
Because I'm still there, aren't I? At university.

LUCY. Oh yeah.

MARK. But I do have a lot. I can show you sometime if you
like.

LUCY. You're alright.

*There's a long, awkward pause. Both are working out how to
continue.*

MARK. Do you – do you read much?

LUCY (*a cold laugh*). Do I read much?

MARK. Yes.

Pause. She laughs again, shakes her head.

What? What is it?

LUCY. It's just. Do you really care if I read much, Mark?

MARK. I'm just /

LUCY. I mean, are you actually really interested in my reading habits?

MARK. I don't /

LUCY. Could you actually, when push comes to shove, give a flying shit if I read anything at all?

MARK. –

LUCY. Maybe I can't even read.

MARK. –

LUCY. Maybe I'm one of those people who looks normal but, like, can't even spell the word 'potato'.

LUCY holds an imaginary crayon and, in a horrible 'spastic' voice, starts spelling the word out.

P…

MARK. Lucy, I don't /

LUCY. O…

MARK. Where's this [come from?]

LUCY. T…

MARK. Come on, stop it now.

LUCY. A… T…

She stops and smiles at him and then stops smiling at him. He's naturally a little freaked out.

MARK. I'm sorry I – I didn't mean to say the wrong [thing]. I just thought it would be nice to – to get to know you.

LUCY. First, you mean?

MARK. No, just…

LUCY. Just what?

MARK. Just – in general. Just *because*.

LUCY. Because what?

MARK. Because you seem like a nice person. *Jesus*.

   Pause.

LUCY. Alright then, tiger. Let's play, um, 'Five Questions'.

MARK. What's that?

LUCY. It's a game. That I've just invented.

MARK. And what happens in this game?

LUCY. You ask me five questions.

MARK. And then what?

LUCY. And then I answer them.

MARK. And then what?

LUCY. And then – I dunno – then you get to fuck my brains out. Look, do you want to just – ask me something, big boy. Anything. Come on.

MARK. Okay. Um. Alright let's… um… What's your name?

LUCY. I've told you my name.

MARK. No but your full name. Surnames and middle names and.

LUCY. That's your first question?

MARK. That's my first question.

LUCY. Because you only have five questions, you know?

MARK. That's my first question.

LUCY (*quietly*). Lucy Ethel Strawbridge.

MARK. Pardon?

LUCY. Lucy Ethel Strawbridge.

MARK (*toying*). One more time, I'm a little deaf in my left…

LUCY. Lucy Ethel Strawbridge.

Beat.

MARK (*teasing*). That's lovely /

LUCY. Fuck off! Just fuck off!

MARK. Lucy *Ethel* Strawbridge, no really that's /

LUCY. Don't be a knobhead.

MARK. No, I mean it – it's very…

LUCY. Urgh, you're such a… Look, my parents had a sadistic
streak when it came to middle names. Argh, I don't want to
play this game /

MARK. Oh no, come on, I'm only… right, next question, right?
What – what did you study at university?

LUCY. I did History of Art.

MARK. Interesting.

LUCY. But I didn't finish it.

MARK. Oh. Why not?

LUCY. Because I had a breakdown and then my tutor came on
to me in a one-to-one and I stabbed him in the leg.

MARK. –

LUCY. Joke!

MARK (*a little freaked out*). Right… ha, very good.

Beat.

Um okay. Next question. Um. What's your best childhood
memory?

She's smiling but she's a little bit thrown by this question.

LUCY. Um, alright, shit. I can't [think of]…

MARK. Just anything, it doesn't have to be /

LUCY. No, it's… Um. Alright. It's a Saturday morning in, like,
March and I'm, um, seven or eight. And it's just this really
nothing-y weekend so, like, my dad and my brother will go
off to Argyle and I'll have to go round Debenhams with my

mum. And I remember I'm watching *CD:UK* on the telly with my brother and my mum comes in and she's like 'sod this, let's go to Alton Towers'. And my brother and me just look at each other because – because my family's quite religious and, not only has she just said 'let's go to Alton Towers' but my world has just been blown wide open by hearing my mum say the word 'sod' for the first time. So um – so we all pile in the car and she makes my dad drive us all the way to – I dunno – wherever Alton Towers is and we get there and – and it's only fucking shut. Because it's March and /

MARK (*laughing*). Oh no.

LUCY. And my parents don't – I mean, who would think that Alton Towers is fucking shut in March? So – so we have to go to, like, Birmingham Aquarium and look at the Portuguese man-o'-wars instead but – but it doesn't really matter because... (*Stops at this point, kind of lost in some painful thoughts.*) Yeah.

Beat.

MARK. Alright, fourth question. (*Beat.*) Why were you drinking by yourself in The Fortescue on a Friday night?

LUCY. Because I was on the hunt for a slightly paunchy, forty-something university lecturer who knows his way around a sausage casing. Next.

MARK. Thirty-nine actually but. Okay. Um, final question then. (*Beat.*) Why – why did you pour your drink away?

LUCY. –

MARK. In the pub. I saw you pour it away. I went to the bogs and I looked back and I saw you tipping it under the banquette.

There's a moment of eye contact. She's weighing something up. The moment passes. She starts rifling through his CDs.

LUCY. Do you have any music that isn't, like, shit. Fucking *Now That's What I Call Stuck in the Mid-Fucking Eighties*?

MARK. Sorry?

LUCY. Fucking like, what is this? Some kind of Dad-Rock
Drivetime wank or. Whitesnake... The Best of Foreigner...
fucking. I mean, fuckin' hell.

Beat.

MARK. I'm terribly sorry. I'll just pop out and buy some –
some emo. Or – or.

LUCY (*amused*). Or?

MARK. Or – I have no idea. (*Beat.*) Do you want another
drink?

LUCY. Sure.

MARK. What do you want?

LUCY. I don't mind.

MARK. Do you like Scotch? I can't imagine you like Scotch.

LUCY. I like Scotch.

MARK. You like Scotch?

LUCY. Uh-huh.

MARK. You've never had Scotch, have you?

LUCY. Um, I so have actually.

MARK. Um, you so haven't.

LUCY. Fuck off!

MARK. You fuck off. Won't be a sec.

*He goes out. When he's gone, LUCY takes a small camera
out of her bag. She starts taking pictures of the room. When
he comes back in the room, he sees what she is doing. She
doesn't notice him until she's put the camera away.*

Hook-a-duck.

LUCY. –

MARK. Hook-a-duck.

LUCY. –

MARK. You said earlier you'd never won anything but you
must have won at hook-a-duck?

LUCY. –

MARK. At the fair?

LUCY. –

MARK. Jesus, where were you [brought up]? You have a hook and there's all these ducks and you use the hook to hook a [duck].

LUCY. Okay.

MARK. And then you win a prize.

LUCY. What kind of prize?

MARK. Um, I dunno, a cuddly toy or a small plastic – *thing*, that's not the – the point is – what is the point? – the point is that it's a prize every time.

LUCY. Gotcha. (*Remembering the thread*.) Oh but that's not winning then, is it? That's just, like, the Taking Part. Which is obviously just bullshitty bullshit, y'know?'

MARK. Is it?

LUCY. Yeah. It's like all those fucking – 'ooh, I've run half a mile in my bra and knickers for charity, here have a medal', 'ooh I've drawn a picture of an African goat, here have a GSCE'? It's just so…

MARK. Bit harsh.

LUCY. No but I mean – it's just so – how – how can we ever progress, y'know? How can we ever – I dunno – *move forward* if there's just all these layers of just –

MARK. Bullshit?

LUCY. Yeah.

MARK. I see.

Beat.

You're very forthright.

LUCY. AKA gobby.

MARK. No, I like it.

LUCY (*dismissive*). Right.

MARK. No, I mean it. You're very…

LUCY. Yeah.

A pause. Something has passed between them.

I love that word. 'Banquette.' Anything that's got a 'bonk' in it.

MARK. Ha.

LUCY. Like, it's one of those words that… only a British person would have thought of such an entirely unsexy word for sex, y'know? Bonk. 'Fancy a bonk?' Pathetic.

MARK. What do you prefer then?

LUCY. Mm, I dunno. Shag.

Fuck.

This bit should be silly but also a tiny bit sexy as well.

Root.

Bone.

Plough.

Ball.

Bang.

Pause.

Have you got a boner?

MARK. What?!

LUCY. You heard me. Have you?

MARK. No! (*He has.*)

LUCY. God, I wish I was a man sometimes. It must be so weird when, like, even saying the word 'plough' can give you a stiffy.

MARK. You say 'like' an awful lot, do you know that?

Pause.

Did you know there's a fish that spends its whole life living in between the tentacles of the Portuguese man-o'-war?

LUCY. I did not.

MARK. They've done these tests and – and even if this fish touched one of these tentacles for the split of a second, it would be instantly paralysed and literally turn to stone. They spend their whole lives darting death by a fraction of a millimetre but still – there's something that draws these fish to make their homes in-between the tentacles. And nobody really knows why.

Beat.

LUCY. Fish are fucking stupid.

MARK *laughs at this.*

MARK. When I was a boy I was so scared of jellyfish that I refused to go in the sea until my dad had /

LUCY starts to kiss MARK. They get off for a while. As things get more intense, one of the glasses spills onto the floor.

Oh shit.

LUCY. Leave it.

MARK. No, it's just /

LUCY. Leave it.

They carry on for several moments until MARK pulls away.

MARK. It's just – you have to – before it…

He comes back with a cloth and starts dabbing at the rug.

LUCY. God, you're weird.

MARK. Me?

LUCY. You.

MARK. How? I'm possibly the least weird person I've ever come across.

LUCY. You're worried about a little spill but it doesn't bother you going home with a strange young woman who tips her drinks under *banquettes*, suggesting she's not as drunk as you'd hoped she was.

MARK. Ah, good point.

She goes towards him.

LUCY. Doesn't that make you just a little bit nervous?

MARK. Not really. I figure even if you've slipped a roofie in my drink and are planning to rape me then that's fine.

She laughs at this. They start kissing again. There's a natural break.

LUCY. Roofie?

MARK. It means Rohypnol.

LUCY. I know that. I didn't expect you to.

MARK. Oh, we have Rohypnol in Plymouth now. All the rage. Rohypnol and meow meow and um /

LUCY. Shut up.

They resume kissing. A pause.

I've been watching you.

MARK. Yes. I know.

LUCY. No, I mean. Not in the pub. I mean – for a while.

MARK. I know.

LUCY. Do you?

MARK. Yes.

There's a pause whilst they both digest this information. LUCY *pulls away.*

LUCY. Did you know that starfish are the only fish with actual real-life testicles?

MARK. No, I did not know that.

LUCY. Ha.

MARK. Real-life testicles you say?

LUCY. Yep.

Beat.

MARK. Testicles like human testicles?

LUCY. Big old hairy fish bollocks.

MARK. Interesting.

LUCY. I know!

MARK. Because /

LUCY. Here we go.

MARK. Because I was under the impression – and I'm only a
    marine scientist so I could be entirely off-base here but – but
    I was under the impression that starfish possess – although
    being gonochoric, of course – that is to say available in both
    male and female flavours – that starfish possess discreetly
    concealed gonads which release their gametes through
    gonoducts located at the vertices of the arms rather than, as
    you say, a pair of hairy low-hangers. Also – and here again,
    I'm willing to be corrected – but I thought that starfish –
    having no discernable vertebrae to speak of – weren't
    actually fish but in fact belong to that spiny-skinned family
    of creatures known as echinoderms. (*Beat.*) But, as I say, I'm
    just throwing ideas out there so.

LUCY (*a compliment*). Dickhead.

*LUCY starts to get off with him again. Things get
    increasingly intense – perhaps a few pieces of clothing are
    awkwardly dispatched – but there's something too frantic
    and jarring about it. LUCY pulls back but MARK wants to
    keep going. After some time, LUCY pulls back again.*

MARK. What?

LUCY. You're not – you're not even [hard]. (*Laughs.*) God.

Beat.

MARK. Are you [laughing at me]? Wow.

Beat.

LUCY. No, hey come on. (*Trying to get back into it but in quite
    a horrible way.*) Come on, just… Let's go. Come on. Come
    on. Please. Please just.

*LUCY is kissing MARK and touching him, pleading with
    him, but in an increasingly aggressive way – pawing at him*

essentially. MARK *tries to stop it several times and eventually has to do it quite forcefully. Perhaps he has to restrain her for a moment.*

MARK. Stop.

A pause. They look at each other. Neither knows how to proceed. LUCY *is clearly humiliated. Suddenly, she makes to leave.*

Hey hey. No, don't. Come on.

LUCY. –

MARK. Hey, I'll – I'll – come on – I'll find us some drinks. Some water or. Come on, please. And we can talk or – just stay there. Please.

MARK *leaves and* LUCY *stands there for a moment. She looks around the room and suddenly the moment overwhelms her. It's a quiet, intensely private moment of despair. When* MARK *re-enters, she's just coming out of it.*

I think our plumbing's fucked so ignore the phytoplankton swimming in the bottom of the… Are you okay?

LUCY *nods.*

You're – you look freezing. Come on.

He sits her down, finds a throw and wraps it around her, and hands her a glass of water. It's quite a lovely gesture. He sits down beside her. Several moments pass.

It's something to do with the house I think. (*Beat.*) I thought it was something to do with me for a while but it's not, is it?

LUCY *is staring straight ahead, almost as if she's not listening. Then she looks at him.*

At first, I thought you might have been a private investigator. (*Small laugh.*) That maybe Laura had, um, hired you to spy on me for the divorce settlement. But then I remembered that she didn't actually give a shit so… And, I mean as much as I would like to think that you're, like, some /

LUCY. 'Like'?

MARK. As much as I would like to think that you're some sort of spy sent by Newcastle University to steal my potentially game-changing research into the effects of ocean acidification on parasitic barnacles, but I don't think that's – I don't think that's a thing either, is it?

Pause.

LUCY. No, probably not.

MARK. How long have you been doing it?

She just looks at him.

When you started, when I first saw you sitting in that rusty-looking Citroën Dolly – which, heads-up, isn't exactly the most discreet spy vehicle – when I first saw you, you were reading something Russian – *Master and Margarita*, wasn't it? – and then you finished that and moved on to Italo Calvino, but you gave up on that probably when you realised it was actually mind-bendingly tedious and now – now you're halfway through the latest Jonathan Franzen. So I would say... three weeks?

LUCY. He was my brother. The boy that died here.

MARK. Yes, I gathered that.

A beat. LUCY *is sizing him up.*

LUCY. Not such a pretty face.

MARK. I think the phrase is 'not just a pretty face' but anyway.

A pause.

Fuck. That's fucking [mad].

LUCY. Yep.

There's a pause in which neither quite knows how to proceed. Finally, MARK *goes to comfort her but she rejects this. Perhaps a little too forcefully. She gets up and starts aimlessly sifting through his stuff.*

Were the floorboards like this when you bought the house?

MARK. Um.

LUCY. Yeah, I imagine there was some gross seventies carpet, probably brown or or purple with, like, a really thick *shag* and, like, that weird wallpaper with all the ridges and when /

MARK. Lucy /

LUCY. When you moved in here with your wife – it's a shame she's left you, by the way, she's very pretty – albeit in a mummy's-let-herself-go-just-a-teensy-bit sort of way – when you moved in here with your wife and probably the baby was already on the way and /

MARK. Lucy /

LUCY. When you moved in here, I bet you thought 'rip it out', 'rip it all out and it will be gone'. All the sadness, all the filthy fucking… Farrow and Ball the living shit out of it and it'll be good as new, fresh as a pin or something.

MARK. Come on.

LUCY. And I bet it was a snip, wasn't it? I bet Mr Marine Biologist and Mrs Marine Biologist couldn't believe their fuckin' luck when they saw the price of it. A house like this, round here? Small issue of the – (*Mouths it.*) d–e–a–d–b–o–y but every house has its problems, eh? Bit of dry rot here, bad paint job there. Previous owner put in PVC when you really wanted original sash. Nothing insurmountable, nothing that can't be gutted, nothing you can't just *rip* out.

MARK. Lucy /

LUCY. And the schools! Have you seen the schools, Mrs Marine Biologist? Ofsteds like a baby's arm holding a blood orange.

MARK. Oi!

LUCY *is finally silent. They look at each other.*

I'm sorry but I don't know what you want.

Beat.

What do you want?

LUCY *laughs at the impossibility of articulating what she wants. A pause. She has found a Transformers toy in a toybox and starts absently playing with it.*

Lucy, are you – are you alright?

Beat.

LUCY. Did you ever see your dad's cock?

MARK. I don't /

LUCY. All my friends, they saw their dad's willies – I mean
only in the shower or in – in passing not y'know up close,
not in a [dodgy] way but we /

MARK. Lucy /

LUCY. We were a very modest family – like, when they needed
a photograph of Richard for the… there were hardly any
because we never did family portraits or… And all my
friends had seen their dad's – it's not like I had an
abnormally strong urge to see my father's dick, you know.
So – so I asked Richard – sorry, that's the dead brother – I
asked Richard if he would show me his penis. I was only
nine so… And he just laughed. I think he thought anything I
said was quite cute, even when I was basically saying 'show
us yer knob'. And that was that morning and then… so
basically my last words to my brother were 'please can I see
your penis?' (*A sad laugh.*) Which is quite weird really.

Beat.

Shall we have another go? I promise not to… I could suck
you off or – or you could just… We could just…

LUCY *has pretty much run out of steam. She just stands
there, helpless, fiddling with the toy. Eventually,* MARK *gets
up. He gently takes the toy from her.*

Do you think a house has a memory? Do you think it
remembers, like on some – fuck, I dunno – some sub-particle
level?

MARK. A sub-particle level?

LUCY. Yeah, fuck off, you know what I mean.

MARK. Yeah, I do. (*Beat.*) But no, I don't.

LUCY. No, me neither. I think that's bullshit, I really do. But I –
I feel very overwhelmed, being here. (*Beat.*) I would also

like to say that I'm not normally such a crazy psycho bitch.
Not – totally anyway.

Pause.

Can I ask you a question?

MARK. Go on.

LUCY. Do you think it's sort-of the reason – or part of the
reason – your wife left? Because of the house?

MARK. Wow, that's [full-on]. Okay, um. (*Thinks.*) No. My wife
left because she was bored of parasitic barnacles. Plus her
mother hates me. Plus it can be really fucking quiet around
here. I mean, I like that. I like the pubs and the beaches
and…

LUCY. And she didn't?

MARK. No, I mean, she did but – but Laura never really – I
guess she never belonged here, you know? When we lived in
London, she was always so busy – we both were. And then
we got here and Hector was born and she – she threw herself
into decorating the house. And then she finished decorating
the house and then… Then I guess we didn't have much to
say to each other after that.

Silence.

What was he like, your brother?

LUCY. What was he like?

MARK. Yes.

Pause. It takes a while for LUCY *to formulate an answer.*

LUCY. He was very – nice. I can only tell you from the
perspective of a nine-year-old girl but… He had this really
soft hair that I was, like, really jealous of. Like, in all
fairness, it should have been girl's hair /

MARK. Yeah.

LUCY. And – he liked taking photographs. He wanted to be a
photographer, an artist. He could make my mum laugh like –
there's this famous family story where he made her laugh so
hard that she actually pissed her knickers. Only a little bit

but. And his favourite meal was ham, egg and chips. They thought he'd run away at first so every night I'd make Mum make ham, egg and chips for tea. So that the smell would, like, waft down the street. Like in the /

MARK. Bisto ad.

LUCY. Yeah. (*Pause*.) What a dickhead.

MARK. Did you – did you know what was going on…

LUCY. At the time?

MARK. Yeah.

LUCY. I think so. It's quite hard now to work out what I knew and what I – I mean, my parents tried to – they tried to shield me from, like, the attention and what-have-you but, like, at school, it was like their Princess Diana moment, y'know?

MARK. Yeah.

LUCY. He became, like, a kind of god. And all these girls who he thought were right dickheads were, like, crying and writing poems about him. (*Beat*.) There was a sponsored walk in his honour…

MARK. Jesus.

LUCY. And I was kind-of famous in my school but as a claim to fame, it doesn't really… 'There's that girl whose brother was found in a sex dungeon.' It doesn't really –

MARK. No.

Beat.

LUCY. I mean, there was no sex dungeon or… They think he probably had this massive asthma attack or.

MARK. Yeah.

LUCY. But when the police came round, they found all these, like, art books – quite hardcore stuff and – and the papers tried to make out that the guy was, like – this – this *paedo-bondage master* who had, like, *corrupted* Richard. And Richard was seventeen so – and they were having sex so – so that was, like, *statutory rape* back then but.

MARK. Shit yeah.

LUCY. And everyone round here – my parents and – they still
totally believe that he – he, like, killed Richard even
though… But I read the court transcripts a few years ago and
he – the guy – he said that Richard used to come round here
all the time. Just to hang out and. And he said that they were
friends but then there was this one time when Richard made
some kind of – because Richard was probably sort-of curious
and I think he was kind-of reaching out. And then they
became sort-of [lovers]. And I remember reading that – he
said that together they both just felt – I dunno – just a little
bit less lost.

MARK. And do you believe that?

LUCY *thinks for a moment, exhales and shrugs. A pause.*

Are your parents – do they still live round here?

LUCY. God, no. Day I left for university, put the house on the
market. Moved to Ireland. Mum died last year. Cancer-slash-
long-term-broken-heart.

Beat.

I was sorting through some of my mum's stuff recently and I
found these photographs, ones that Richard had taken when
he was… obviously. Like, just pictures of his friends or
people on the street or. And some of them are quite – I mean,
I don't know about photography but some of them are quite
– quite beautiful really. I was thinking I might send them to a
publisher or…

MARK. You should.

LUCY. I thought at first there'd be loads of Richard but there's
not because, well, because he's taking them – duh. But there
is one of him. (*Beat.*) He's sitting just there – (*Indicates the
place.*) When you went out, I recognised the cornicing – or
coving or… He's pulling this really stupid face – he always
did this like – (*Pulls face.*) in photographs. (*Beat.*) But he
looks – yeah.

Another pause.

I think I kind-of hated him actually. Or – the memory of him.
Never said that before. I used to get these – when I was, like,

fourteen, I had this massive fuck-off fringe that I could sort-of hide behind and because I had this fringe, I used to get these really pussy spots just here – (*Indicates place*) and I just sort-of wanted to – to disappear. Because it just overshadowed… everything. It was just this big – shadow. And you try and run away from it but it never… Because it's not something you can ever – change. There's nothing you can – do with it. And you try ignoring it and then you try not ignoring it but it's all just…

Another pause.

I've spent so long imagining just… what it's like in here.

MARK. And – what is it like?

Beat.

LUCY. It's just a room.

Long pause.

MARK. Hector was born here. In here, you know?

LUCY. Seriously?

MARK. Yeah. Laura wanted a water birth – obviously – and um… (*Indicates a place.*) Paddling pool. Buckets of warm water. Enya's Greatest Hits in the background. And then – and then Hector.

MARK *is smiling.*

Course no one ever tells you what to do with the paddling pool afterwards. (*Grimacing.*) Looked like some kind of crime scene or – (*Realising what he's just said.*) oh, shit.

LUCY (*laughing at the awfulness of what he's just said*). No, it's –

MARK. Bollocks, sorry. (*Laughing as well.*) I really meant that as a [good memory].

LUCY. Yeah, I know. (*Beat.*) And – it is.

Pause.

MARK. Do you want to – do you want to see more – of the house? You could…

She thinks for a moment then shakes her head. Pause.

LUCY. You – you have to find a way to live with it, don't you?

Pause. Neither of them move.

(*Collecting herself.*) Are you going to stay here or?

MARK. Um, I don't know, to be honest. I mean, I'm going to
stick in Plymouth – I actually really love it – there's a certain
kind of light on the ocean here that... But Laura's moving
back to London with – with Hector. Wants to get the place
valued so... That's why it's so tidy. Should have seen it last
week. I'm not very good with domestic stuff.

LUCY. I am. I actually *like*, like, housework. I'm surprisingly
good with a Swiffer.

He gives her a sceptical look.

What? Fuck off, I am!

Pause.

Would it not be weird?

MARK. What?

LUCY. Being in this house without...

MARK. Without Laura and Hector?

LUCY. Yeah.

MARK (*thinks*). Yeah, probably. (*Beat.*) What do you think I
should [do]?

Pause.

LUCY. I think you should stay. This is – this is where you live.

Pause.

MARK. Gonna go away for a few weeks anyway. Look for
paddleworm samples in Norfolk. Clear my head.

LUCY. That sounds nice.

MARK. I think it will be. (*Beat.*) You should – you should
come.

LUCY. Nah.

MARK. I mean it. I think – I think I could do with a mate right now. Come.

LUCY. Nah.

Pause.

Yeah?

MARK. Yeah. You can – you can hold my equipment.

He gives her a look.

LUCY. Dickhead.

Pause.

MARK. What do you want to do now?

LUCY. Quite hungry actually.

MARK. Yeah, I could probably poke something down.

LUCY. Could I have some toast please?

MARK. Sure. One toast coming right up.

MARK *leaves.* LUCY *sits on the sofa, thinking. After several moments, she starts rifling through* MARK*'s CDs. She finds a song she likes and puts it on at a relatively low volume. It's a big, euphoric power ballad by one of the bands mentioned earlier.* MARK *returns with a plate of toast.*

Rumbled.

LUCY. What?

MARK. Admit it. This music. You like it, don't you?

LUCY (*laughing*). Fuck off.

He hands her some toast. He turns the music up a bit.

MARK. Go on. Just say it.

LUCY *gives him a look.*

Go on.

Beat. He's gradually turning it up.

Say it and I'll turn it up.

Beat.

Say it and I'll turn it up really loud.

By now, the music is quite deafening.

Just say you like it and I'll turn it up loud enough to – to drown it all out. Everything!

Beat.

Go on!

Pause.

LUCY. I fucking love it!

The music does indeed drown everything out in quite a giddy way. LUCY *stands there, taking the music in, while* MARK *moves to the sofa.* LUCY *laughs, turns to* MARK *and says something.* MARK *smiles, takes a piece of toast and starts eating it.*

Sudden fade.

www.nickhernbooks.co.uk

 facebook.com/nickhernbooks

 twitter.com/nickhernbooks